Don't Quit!

You Can Achieve Your Set Goals and Dreams

By:

K. Dennis Chiedu

Don't Quit!

Keli and Josh Ventures, PO Box 770023, Houston TX 77215, or contact by email at kandjventures04@gmail.com

Unless otherwise indicated, all Scripture quotations are taken from the New American Standard Version of the Holy Bible – The Open Bible Expanded Edition, by The Lockman Foundation.

ISBN 13: 978-0-692-02860-5

DEDICATION

To the Holy Spirit –
My Guide, Helper, Teacher and Comforter.

TABLE OF CONTENTS:

ACKNOWLEDGEMENTS

I wish to thank Mrs. S. U. Ogbuoji, whom God used to motivate me to get my ideas together and putting my writing skills to work. Your support is appreciated very much. May God bless you, your nice and lovely family.

My thanks also go to my late mom, Mrs. Felicia Kenechukwu – *nwabugo*, who was a source of light and encouragement. Whenever things got so rough she was there for me. You are an inspiration even today. Though dead, your legacy lives on!

To my friends and brethren, I say a big thank you and God bless. I love you all.

I want to thank my pastor, Dr. Dan Onuoha for writing the foreword for this book, and Ms. Elizabeth Westbrook for carefully reading through and editing the manuscript. May God keep blessing you and enable you to continue to bless others.

Most of all my thanks go to the Almighty God who keeps inspiring me and has helped me package this book. No one could have done this work if not for God. To God alone be all the glory, adoration, honor, power, dominion, thanks and praise forever – Amen.

INTRODUCTION

Many people oftentimes awaken with wonderful dreams and ideas. Full of zeal and vigor, they begin to work towards accomplishing them. But when enthusiasm begins to wane along the line, they step back and drag their feet. When you ask them what the problem is, they point to one obstacle after another with no definitive way of overcoming them. As a result, some out rightly quit trying, and think that there is no other way to get this thing done.

The message of this book is this, "You can get beyond any obstacle you face by the power of God! God knows that obstacles will appear on your way to fulfilling your dreams and destiny, but He has equipped you with what you may need along the way to achieving them. God has given you the intellect, strength, wisdom, hunger, desire and other gifts to accomplish this. Today the Holy Spirit is living in you if you are a child of God. However, you need patience, focus and determination to keep going and see results. Your focus must be on the promises of God. When God was speaking to Abraham, the father of our faith in the book of Genesis, He told him that He would give him land as far as his eyes could see (Genesis 13:14-15). Abraham was so determined not to give up; his persistence helped him receive all God promised him. Abraham, our father of faith was faced with his own difficulty, but he depended absolutely on God for his own establishment, and for a son who would be his heir. If you look closely at his life, you will see his determination to receive God's blessings. According to the Bible, at God's instance, Abraham left the place where he settled with his father who was Terah of Haran to go to a land where the foundation and builder was God (Genesis Chapter 12:1-4). He waited on God for direction; he trusted Him for protection, provision and more. It is pertinent for us to come to terms with what the Bible was making reference to when it said that Abraham trusted God. It means that Abraham cast himself on God. Put in another way, Abraham offered himself [*like an offering*] to God. At this very point, he no longer had a mind of his own but the mind of God. Abraham began to accept every word that God spoke as being the final authority. In doing this, Abraham became a friend of God, and as a result God paid him a visit and also got his opinion before taking a final decision on matters that pertained to the land of Sodom and Gomorrah. All the challenges Abraham saw along the way could not stop him from looking ahead, and when the fullness of time came, God mightily blessed him. Not only did God bless Abraham with Isaac, the child of his dreams, He also elevated him to the status of being His friend. Such privilege and honor was given to none other. If not that he had resolved to reach the end with God, he would have quit along the way. But Abraham was firm in his faith in God. You also can reach such a height if you persevere and if you whole heartedly trust God to keep His promises and covenants towards you.

Elisha was also able to receive the double portion he requested from Elijah his master because he was determined and focused on receiving that desire despite his discouragements. **2 Kings 2:9-10 (NASB)** says, ***"When they had crossed over, Elijah said to Elisha, 'Ask what I shall do for you before I am taken from you.' And Elisha said, 'Please, let a double portion of your spirit be upon me.' He said, 'You have asked a hard thing. Nevertheless, if you see me when I am taken from you, it shall be so for you;'..."*** Elisha refused to accept every entreaty from Elijah to go back. Elisha knew what he wanted, pursued it, waited, was focused and persevered. Despite all odds, eventually Elisha got what he wanted. You can too!

The question you need to ask yourself is this: "Is my dream also God's dream?" Other important questions are: "What are the reasons behind my dream? Are my motives selfish, or are they embedded in God's plan for my life and generation?" As long as your dream is God-inspired and you stay committed and focused to seeing it through, surely you will get there because God will also be there to see it accomplished. God said to the Prophet Jeremiah, ***"I am watching over My word to perform it [carry it out, or execute it]."*** **(Jeremiah 1:12[NASB])** That promise is also applicable to you today because God is no respecter of persons. If He could do that for the prophet, He will do the same for you for His glory. You need to come to the understanding that obstacles are temporal and that God has given you the power and the ability under His anointing to pull down and deal with every challenge that comes across your path to your vision. Obstacles are pivotal points for you to show what you are made of and God is counting on you to overcome every one of them. The Apostle Paul in his second letter to the Corinthians 4:18 said that the obstacles seen are temporal, but the blessings yet to be seen but confirmed by God's word are eternal. Those promises in God's word are not mere words; they are more tangible than the obstacles staring at you. They are backed up by God Himself. When you understand the personality of God you value them. Each country's currency is backed up by what they call the gold reserve in the treasury. That is exactly the way it is with the word of God. The personality of God is a back-up to His word. Can God do what He said? Absolutely! God was just breathing Himself on those pages through His spirit so we can run with them. The Apostle encourages us to be more courageous as we meet those challenges along the way.

"Therefore we do not lose heart, but though our outer man is decaying, yet our inner man is being renewed day-by-day. For momentary, light affliction is producing for us eternal weight of glory, while we look not at the things which are seen, but at the things which are not seen; for the things which are seen are temporal, but the things which are not seen are eternal." **(2 Corinthians 4:16-18 [NASB])**

Another important thing here is the need for consistency in our commitment to the vision we pursue notwithstanding the challenges we face. You need to speak life to your vision and stay at it. You also need to work towards actualizing your vision. Joseph was a good example in this respect. He had a dream of becoming the leader and deliverer of his people, but out of jealousy and envy his brethren plotted to stop that dream. Knowing that the dream was God's design for him, Joseph never gave up hope. He stayed focused and determined to succeed. This was a form of challenge on his path but he never wavered nor stopped being hopeful; he kept talking and visualizing his dreams. Even while in prison the same attitude and commitment followed him. The reason is that everywhere Joseph found himself he was conscious of his dreams. It affected his conduct and behavior. He never lost who he was even when the high-road lifestyle he chose to live landed him in prison. Joseph did not allow this challenge to bother nor sway him. He accepted his obstacles and went on to interpret other people's dreams for them thus giving their life meaning. With strong conviction and understanding, Joseph knew that someday he would be leaving prison to fulfill his own destiny. His life story is proof that the earnest and consistent expectations of the righteous cannot be cut short.

The obstacles and setbacks Joseph encountered could neither dim nor stop his vision. His dream eventually materialized and became fulfilled. He later became a deliverer and leader of his people. The lesson in the story of Joseph is that irrespective of the difficulties and challenges to achieving your dreams Beloved, "Don't Quit". Your expectations are guaranteed and assured by God. God does not give you dreams which you cannot achieve. Whatever dreams He gives, He will provide for every need to get the dreams accomplished. You may want to ask what your role is in fulfilling your God given dreams. All you need to do is discover what God wants you to do and make up your mind that you will not quit.

The challenges of life are opportunities to build us up and get us equipped for future challenges in life. Apostle Paul said in his first letter to the Corinthians 10:13 that with such temptations God provides a way of escape. But to escape and overcome the challenges, you have to be bold and assertive. You need to stand firm in faith and command those challenges to move, and you also should believe that they have no choice but to obey you. In Proverbs 28:1 (NASB), the Bible says, *"The wicked flee when no one is pursuing, but the righteous are bold as a lion."* This passage is telling us what it takes to get to fulfill our dreams. It is telling us that for our dreams to come true, it takes boldness, courage, and an unwavering determination.

"Fixing our eyes on Jesus, the author and perfecter of [our] faith who for the joy set before Him endured the cross, despising the shame, and has sat down at the right hand of the

throne of God. For consider Him who also endured such hostility by sinners against Himself, so that you may not grow weary and lose heart." Hebrew 12:2-3 (NASB).

Was it not that Jesus kept His eyes focused on His mission and the outcome, He would have derailed. So, in addition to determination and courage, focus is also very essential to getting things done. This scripture encourages us to follow after [*emulate*] such men who through faith obtained the promises and accomplished their goals and dreams. It also enjoins us to emulate our Lord and Savior Jesus Christ who was so obsessed with His mission that death became ordinary to Him. He also endured many other forms of afflictions from men in order to get His mission accomplished.

The power of focus is very important to accomplish any dream, vision or task. If Jesus had to focus and endure to get His mission accomplished, we much more should do the same if we want to fulfill our dreams. There is no pass here friend; we need to learn to avoid all manner of distractions towards our dreams and tasks. You should understand that although He is the Son of God, Jesus became entirely human when He was here on earth. He experienced what other humans experienced yet He never gave up His vision nor abandoned His mission. He patiently endured all pains and sufferings. When we become determined and have focus towards our dreams, every challenge that comes our way becomes small before us, and also serves as opportunity for our lifting, shinning and honor.

Can you see the good hidden in your challenges? You may say, "Dennis there's no good in suffering, and I want it all easy." Nothing good, comes easy my friend. Every great prize is attained at great cost and great sacrifice. Those who go to the Olympics and shine celebrate and flaunt their medals, paid heavily behind the scenes to celebrate in the open. They did not just go out and win a medal. They trained, suffered, denied themselves of some comfort, persevered, focused and were determined to succeed. That was why it was all joy when they made it and they saw their dreams come true. You need to realize that all things work together for good to them that are called according to God's plan and purpose. No matter the obstacles facing your dream today, make up your mind and let it be settled that you will come out on top, and that your dream will surely be realized. Many people have embarked on some academic journeys and businesses without great bank accounts or loans. Today they have both graduated and own businesses. Some are working in big corporations while others are employing people to work for them!

Beloved, may the good Lord grant you deeper understanding as you read and meditate on the truth revealed in this book. May your inner eyes be opened clearer to comprehend what is required of you to get your dreams accomplished. As you meet various difficulties while you pursue your dreams, may the hand of the Lord be strong upon you to help you be firm and achieve victory over every one of such difficulties in Jesus' name – Amen.

K. Dennis Chiedu

08 – 27 – 12

FOREWORD

Don't quit is an inevitable reading for anyone who has yet to see his light of destiny blink much more shine.

Moments of darkness and hopelessness abound in lives, no wonder many seek for shortcuts which end up as longest ways.

By this book, Isaiah 50:10 is fulfilled, as it is written:

> *"Who among you fears the LORD? Who obeys the voice of His Servant? Who walks in darkness And has no light? Let him trust in the name of the LORD And rely upon his God."*

As challenging as it may appear, I believe this scripture is pungent to life because *Verse 9* is fulfilled, as it is written:

> *"Surely the Lord GOD will help Me; Who is he who will condemn Me?......."*

Until *Verse 10* is fulfilled the appropriate wisdom and power from God for a destiny difference is not released in ones favor.

Therefore it is my submission to say, read 'Don't quit' and receive Grace to trust and rely upon your God for if you refuse to quit your mountain will quit.

Dr. Dan Onuoha
Presiding Bishop
Gracelife Church Worldwide

Chapter I
Reason for Affliction

Whenever God wants to bless, position or lift someone to a higher ground it is like an announcement goes out everywhere- the kind you hear during the wedding ceremony by the officiating priest – "Does anyone have anything to say that will stop this marriage ceremony from proceeding? Speak now, or forever hold your peace." However, unlike the wedding ceremony where everyone pretends that all is well and stays silent, here challenges begin to set in. Oppositions begin to mount in droves. The devil begins to haul all manner of attacks against the individual with the intention to derail their blessing and stop him from reaching his goal. Issue upon issue begins to arise. Damaging accusations also follow. As a result fear and pessimism begin to set in and the individual comes at a loss of what to do next. However, friend, never be too comfortable to remain where you are. Strive to get ahead and reach your goal, and the blessing that God has allotted to you will follow. Work hard to be on the top! In the gospel of Saint John 10:10, Jesus said,

"The thief comes only to steal, kill and destroy…"

This statement shows the entire mission of the devil. He will go to any length to frustrate you. The Devil will employ every tactic and trick. There are no barred areas for him to destroy his victim. He uses fear, embarrassment, intimidation, discouragement and others to hinder one from being blessed and from attaining his set goals.

The devil can comfortably do this and succeed when a believer is not steadfast and strong enough in the word of God and word of faith. The believer may give up and surrender to the evil one. This could manifest in a simple statement being made by the believer such as – "Maybe this (my dream) is not the will of God for me!"

Beloved, God expects us as sons and daughters to stand our ground and lay hold of what belongs to us. When the time came Caleb told Joshua to honor God's promise and give him his portion that Moses promised him after spying out Jericho. Though eighty-five years old at the time, Caleb took the mountain and overthrew the giants occupying the land and took possession of it (Joshua 14:9-12). We will always conquer giants who try to take over our lands and inheritances when we do not give heed to the accusations and attacks of the evil one or when we accept that we are limitless.

The Bible commands us to resist the devil and he will flee from us. Someone likened affliction to examination. He said the moment you scale through it you are no longer on the same level. In fact you will advance some steps up. If you are scared, you either remain at the same place or you depreciate, but once you pass it you get elevated and no longer fear it! The same thing happens when we confront affliction. As long as we are afraid of it, affliction will keep subduing us, but once we take it head on, it bows and the fear vanishes.

One needs to understand that exams signal when you are due for the next level. That is why in some offices and establishments, employees are made to undergo certain trainings and tests. Those that scale through are promoted while the others remain at the same level. This usually occurs when some senior level positions are vacant. Also for a student to be promoted to the next class, the individual has to meet the testing requirements of the exam and secure the passing score as well. During the time of an examination there is difficulty but because you desire to move up, you endure the drills and pass the examination. Therefore, when you see challenges, gird yourself and face the situation squarely, for your accelerating to another level is likely right around the corner. A lot of people have remained at the same place longer than necessary only because they are unable to meet the requirements for the next level. That is the design and desire of the devil for you; not to be able to meet the needed requirements for your blessing or goal. But "Don't Quit!"

The devil wants to use challenges to bog you down and hold you stagnated, but that is not God's plan for you. Since that is not His plan, God wants you to see every challenge as an opportunity to give Him glory, an avenue to take you to the next level by God's grace. You will get a better understanding by examining what the Apostle Paul said in Romans 8:28;

"God causes all things to work for the good of those that love him and are called according to His purpose."

You know, we are usually good at complaining and blaming others for things that happen around us rather than sitting down to solve our problems. The best approach is to have a conversation with God and ask God what lessons are in the challenges you face.

You know what; exams also help one to discover his abilities. Like exams, overcoming challenges help to build up your faith and brace up for another level. In referencing the Apostle Paul, afflictions do or accomplish the same thing for the believer. During the hard times the believer discovers his hidden potential. This discovery and Paul putting his faith into use caused his potential to distinguish him. God usually turns affliction into favor for the benefit of the believer, however, the devil employs it to frustrate his victim.

People do not begin to develop survival instincts until they get pressed to the wall. They do not begin to think and use their creative ability until things get out of hand. Most successful people you know today, have had this experience. If you know one, get closer and ask him how he got where he occupies right now. His stories will encourage you. I remember those days when we were kids after the death of my dad, my mom a primary (elementary) school teacher was faced with uncertainties. She knew her salary would not be enough to feed her kids, clothe them, pay their school fees and meet other needs. Thank God the house we lived in was built by my dad so the issue of rent was taken care of, but these other needs were huge. After thinking of what to do to help her meet her challenge, my mom, in addition to her teaching, decided to engage in part-time petty trading – selling soft drinks, small food items, and other things used in making and cooking soup. In addition to getting extra money from the sales, she used part of the goods to feed her children – an added bonus.

She was not discouraged by her challenges; instead she succeeded in overcoming them to train her seven kids. Today all of them have succeeded: obtaining one degree after another in institutions of higher learning, some holding distinguished positions in society.

That is why I said initially that afflictions or challenges bring out the best in you and help you to discover your potential.

Remember you have a place at the top so you do not need to remain at the bottom of life. Take those difficulties as a ladder to climb up out of life's pit, and not as your mourning site. This is the problem with a lot of folks. Instead of thinking and planning on ways to climb out of their pit of depression, they engage in self-pity.

I heard about a woman whose husband was a multi-millionaire; he virtually did everything for her while he was alive. It was when the man suddenly died that she realized she did not know how to do anything but cook. As she could not manage his estate, the business empire crumbled, but she developed her cooking ability and turned it into a great business. As a result she developed and came to own a chain of restaurants. If not for the circumstance in which she found herself, she would have never discovered her potential. There is nobody that does not have the potential to be great even though it may need to be discovered. Our potential is most often discovered during rough times and when we have become uncomfortable with our current position or situation.

Afflictions may not be personal, but are always about solving problems. The society may be in dire need of something. It is our ability and more so our hunger to solve problems that can bring us lasting rewards. Society will appreciate you; you will become a hero for solving problems. In addition you will benefit financially, socially, politically and more. Your problem solving skills will open diverse doors that ordinarily you would not have been able to enter.

There is significant lesson in the relationship between gold and furnaces. Without the furnace, gold cannot come out as pure and therefore will not appear as luminous limiting its value. Without improving its worth by withstanding the heat of the furnace, gold would not be appreciated nor valued. You see, the impurities that cover the gold are removed during the firing process in the furnace.

Remember also that folks turn in their gold materials sometimes to goldsmiths for refinishing, to restore the beauty and glow of the precious metal when it gets dull. After this, it comes out glowing causing people to rush to get it. Many people love gold and its wares and want it to adorn their world. That also reflects in the pricing and use. Golden materials are used on great occasions.

People who know the true value of gold usually do not adorn them casually.

Like a furnace, affliction extracts the impurities from you. It helps to remove character defects and things that are not useful to your life, while all along bringing out of you those virtues that are beneficial to you and others. Some people are naturally lazy but when they are hit by certain situations, they change for the better. I heard of someone fired from her job for negligence of duty, after passing through some rough experiences over time, eventually she got another one. Come and see her today, she has become the darling of her boss. Why? She now takes her job serious and no longer toys with her duties. That is what affliction can achieve in someone's life. Sometimes affliction is self-imposed, other times it is external, but those that maximize it gain from it while others loose.

From the Holy Bible, we know about the man David, a great king in Israel. We read of the numerous challenges he passed through as a shepherd boy. We saw how he killed a lion and a bear when at different occasions they came to feed on his flock. These were grave challenges, but his victories and the experiences emboldened him. You remember his confession to King Saul when he was readying for a combat with Goliath of Gath,

"The Lord who delivered me from the paw of the lion and from the paw of the bear, He will deliver me from the hand of this Philistine." (1 Samuel 17:37 [NASB]).

In a case of national affliction David came up with the solution and the rest was history. That experience brought David close to King Saul and endeared him to the hearts of his people. The experience he garnered from them also made him an expert and fearless warrior. Even during his reign there was no record of any battle he lost despite fighting numerous wars.

Also, concerning the Lord Jesus, the Bible says in the book of Hebrews 5: 8-9 that He learned obedience through the things He suffered. He also became an eternal source of salvation to those that obey him. What a glory and lifting?! Friend, Jesus' sufferings while here on earth brought Him an unparalleled honor throughout human history.

So, children of God, stop seeing challenges as frustrations, discover opportunities in them. Begin to take them as stepping stones to your glory. Welcome challenges, they can only come to you because you have answers to them. Quit running away when they show up. God is counting on you to fix them as they appear on your path to glory, "Don't Quit!"

However, to achieve this and be in the position to set goals and fulfill your dreams, you need a good knowledge and understanding of the word of God. You will also need strength and good courage. That was exactly what God instructed Joshua when he took over the leadership mantle of His people after the death of Moses. God does not allow anything bigger than you to come your way. If He does allow anything He has already equipped you to handle it!

In 1 Corinthians 10:13, the Bible says that God will provide you a way of escape to enable you to endure and overcome the difficulty. So beloved, do not slap God in the face by treating Him as though he were a liar. We treat God as though he were a liar when we do not stand up to challenges and oppositions that come our way and gain from them. For God to keep backing you up, you will have to develop strong courage and a determined sense of faith as some will say, "get a thick skin." Remember He can only walk with you to the extent you are willing to walk with Him.

God may allow affliction on someone to prevent him from self-destruction. In Psalm 23:3, the Bible says,

"He restored my soul; He leaded me in the paths of righteousness for His name's sake."(KJV)

Sometimes people lose focus while basking in God's benefits. Some, at times forget about God while paying more attention to worldly things they consider more important and more pressing. They begin to center their attention and affection more on the blessings rather than the One that gives the blessing. Things of comfort and success like businesses, marriage and career start taking them away from those things that add to their spiritual development and service to God. At this point the heart of many begins to get far away from God. To them God has become a secondary matter.

When this happens, the love of God compels Him to intervene and get such persons back on track so they do not shipwreck their lives. The Bible says that every good father or parent disciplines the child he loves; so does God our father (Hebrews 12: 4-11). He cannot fold His hands and watch you destroy yourself.

If that is the case, can you imagine what it will look like when God begins to draw your attention by force. I tell you, it is not going to be easy. He can go as far as removing those things that have been drawing you away from Him, depending on how stubborn you prove to be. The children of Israel had this experience several times before the coming of Christ as was recorded in the scriptures. The same still happens today to the people of God when they go wayward.

David said, ***"He restoreth my soul."*** This means to say that God fights to bring you back to Him anytime you wander away. He does not want the enemy to destroy you, so when you step away from grace He comes vigorously looking for you. You belong to Him and He will always want you to be with Him. Therefore, anything that would take you away from Him, He will ensure that it is dealt with seriously. An adage (proverb) has it that it is the grass that suffers when two elephants fight. So brethren, in order to avoid getting it the rough way, always stay where you belong. He will permit anything that will harass you to draw your attention back to Him. You must remember that before it gets to this point, He must have pleaded with you for a long time until you refused to turn back.

So when God begins to bless you, be careful and do not be carried away by the air of that blessing. The repercussion can be bitter if you do so. Always remember God as the source of your blessing. Do not ever try to misappropriate His glory. Simply stated, all you have was given. In Deuteronomy 8:18, the Bible enjoins us always to remember it is the Lord who gave us power to make wealth. What we become in life, despite our efforts, are as a result of His grace and mercy. Some think it is by their connections, knowledge, position or power. It is at this point that many err. Some people think and say they are self-made. I wonder. But that is arrogance and pride, and God detests that. You may have to get away from people who talk that way so you do not learn it and share in their punishment. Always walk in the way God planned for you.

Another reason afflictions arise is to demonstrate God's glory. In John 9: 1-3, the disciples asked Jesus why a certain man was blind. They were curious, perhaps because of the teachings they had been receiving about sin and condemnation from the scribes and Pharisees, juxtaposed to the new message of hope and love Christ had brought them. They wanted to know if the blindness was the result of somebody's sin, but Jesus replied that its purpose was that the power of God may be displayed.

Most of the challenges people face today are there as a result of gross ignorance – not knowing the will of God and what is in it for them. The Bible says; my people are destroyed for a lack of knowledge (Hosea 4:6). It also says that we shall know the truth; the truth we know shall set us free. It is this understanding that gives you leverage over situations. Once you realize what the will of God is for you, with that understanding, and confidence, you can exploit any challenge. Some of those obstacles are there for you as stepping stones to something higher. The devil places them in your life to keep you from maturing spiritually. However, you do not need to succumb to that deceit; your blessings are behind the façade. All you need to do is be patient and persist; then call God's attention to the obstacle. As you do that get ready to spoil the Devil's plans!

Note this friend, I am not saying that affliction is God's will for you. Some teach that, but Christ did not say so; however, it helps you discover God's power and love for you when it shows up. Some challenges are faith provokers. Your faith level and confidence in God increases when you overcome them through His power. God enjoins you to call on Him when you encounter challenges and He promised to deliver.

"And call upon me in the day of trouble; I shall rescue you, and you will honor me." **Psalm 50:15 (NASB)**

Friends, God guarantees you deliverance, *"...I shall rescue you..."* All He wants is the glory.

The next form of affliction is to equip you. I guess this is where those that believe that affliction is God's will for their lives hinge their belief. This type of affliction is like apprenticeship or training.

"He trains my hands for battle, so that my arms can bend a bow of bronze." **Psalm 18:34 (NASB)**

Sometimes when one receives a special assignment from God, the individual is first trained and prepared for the assignment. Most assignments require patience, wisdom, kindness and compassion. Sometimes you discover that affliction has a way of breaking a man and making him imbibe these virtues. In Hebrews 5:8, the Bible says that Jesus learned obedience through the things He suffered.

Also we read about Moses. The Bible made us to understand he trained as a prince in Pharaoh's palace, to lead people to war, but not according to God's plan for his life. As the time for his assignment was fast approaching, God sent him into exile and retrained him, making him meeker than any man who walked the face of the earth.

However, before he went into exile, the Bible recorded that he killed an Egyptian who was maltreating a Jew (Exodus 2: 11-12). When Moses returned, he was a changed person entirely. It got to the point that when God wanted to wipe away the people of Israel in the wilderness due to their stubbornness, it was Moses who pleaded on their behalf for mercy – a big contrast to his hot tempered nature before God touched him during the exile. He became patient and considerate about the result and the impact of that action if taken, which was not the case before.

Another good example here is David. He suffered so much at the hands of King Saul. David kept running from one wilderness place to another and from one cave to the next, hiding from the king. That experience made him tough. He became a tough fighter and warlord. Those experiences made him become a great warrior in his time. It enabled him to subdue his neighbors when he later became the king of Israel. As a result, his people never went into captivity during his reign.

There is something very important here that I want you to see. A shepherd boy became a warrior. Challenges matured him and he seized the opportunity to change his destiny forever. That is what this type of affliction can achieve in the life of an individual.

Anytime you come across challenges in your life journey, it is not a time to quit and run away. Rather it is a time to get back to God, be on your feet and find out what He wants from you. He may need your attention. You need Him to direct you as you go. He only knows what He wants to achieve in your life and through you. A lot of opportunities are missed day by day by those who are not sensitive to the Spirit and those that do not understand signs and times. Perhaps that challenge staring you in the face is there because you are due for the next level. Do not let it go; take advantage of it, "Don't Quit!"

Chapter II
Strategy

Strategy is purely a military term used in warfare to undermine and defeat the enemy to win a war. Strategizing is when an individual sits down to plan towards achieving a desired goal. It involves the setting up of the main vision and the step by step process of accomplishing that dream. Some call it a plan of action to getting a goal achieved, usually over a period of time. It usually takes a long time to bring needed results because it involves the preparation of resources and planning for the use of the resources before, during and after an action. Many people do not know that humanity is in warfare against the forces of this life and nature. They only look at life on the periphery; as a result thinking and planning become stressful to them. On the other hand, successful people are great strategists. They spend time thinking and putting one and one together to achieve what they want. They are usually restless until they get what they want.

Also when one decides on a venture or vision, there is the need to sit down and draw a plan on how to get the dream or goal accomplished. There should be a step by step plan on making sure you are able to accomplish this task, not a situation where after starting you will abandon the mission due to one excuse or another. Today, sports people, business people, politicians and others employ these terms as they execute their various visions. I want also to let you know that some ministers of the gospel equally employ plans and preparation to effectively bring the Good News to the world.

So, for you to succeed in a chosen field, you may have to employ this winning formula for the process to work.

Once you have made up your mind on what to do and set your goal, the next thing is sitting down to plan how to get the mission accomplished with what you have in your possession. Remember Jesus told us that if we must wage a war or build a house, we should ensure that we have enough resources to execute the projects before setting off lest we become a laughing stock when we are not able to break-even (Luke 14:28-32). This advice is also very important as we consider setting out on any mission, as I do not think anyone would like to embark on any unsuccessful venture.

For any government to pride itself on its ability in protecting its people, it must employ good strategies. Many countries that enjoy food and energy securities today took many years to plan and get them working. It was not just a mere wish or wave of wand that got it started. It was deliberate conscious efforts taken by a government and its citizens to ensure they enjoy security in those things that matter most to them. Like in the USA and others, they created what they call "strategic reserves" in different locations of the country to store food and energy against any unforeseen circumstances. When there is abundance, they buy the surplus and store away for that rainy day. Some of these reserves can take years to run out. Sometimes when the world energy cost is high, the government taps into the reserve to cushion the effect of the world market on the local economy. The same thing applies when there is low harvest or famine. The government supports the local market from the reserve. Apart from contributions from people during emergencies, it is usually from the reserve that the government takes some aids to reach out to the victims.

In the book of Genesis Chapter 41, God warned pharaoh against the impending famine coming against his land in seven years. He told pharaoh about the need to prepare against the famine through the dream He gave him during the time of Joseph. Joseph was then a prisoner but through him God revealed the mystery to pharaoh who later gave him charge to execute that dream. For seven years Joseph bought the surplus that was produced in Egypt and strategically placed them as reserves throughout the entire kingdom. That idea was so successful that it not only saved Egypt but the entire region at that time. People came from different places to buy food from Egypt.

This is why thinking and planning is necessary if we want to achieve our goals. For any nation to be strong, it must be able to feed and protect its citizens, but it comes by careful planning and execution.

I remember a very good friend of mine, Chiedu, who after many years of working with the government and in the private sector came to realize that he was aging, and with time may find it difficult to remain employed and meet his family obligations. After careful reflections, Chiedu decided to own what he called "his own business." However, he did not have all it would take to start a good business, like skill sets, capital, the acumen and disposition being a novice. Knowing that he did not have all of these, he sought counsel among close successful business friends. The information he got was very useful.

Not long afterwards, Chiedu went to train as an apprentice in one of the fields he wanted to be. Knowing he did not have the money to finance the entire project, he maintained and did not quit his corporate job. He planned the two activities in such a way that they did not conflict with each other. While managing work and the training he began also to set aside funds to serve as starting capital for the business when it would eventually kick off. In the meantime, he still had a family to maintain and a lot of bills to pay while pursuing his goal. His story is like that of every person with a dream with whom I have had contact. He knew where he wanted to be but not how to get there. It was not an easy task for him, but he was determined to take on the two together until he began to learn the skills he would need to succeed. Initially, it was like learning Greek at an old age to him, but after a while he began to learn and assimilate some of those skills. At first, someone advised Chiedu to go to business school and obtain a degree in entrepreneurship. After much consideration, he found that he still needed hands-on training to really acquire what he needed to run his own business. Still, he does not plan to work for people any more. Chiedu's strategy is a five year plan: to work, train and set aside savings within this period. He is determined and learning fast, hoping to jumpstart the business after this period. This is a form of strategy and realignment.

Another friend of mine – Chyke, owns a vibrant car care shop, but where it is sited does not help him make profits. He stays in a neighborhood that is not affluent or middle class. He has been looking to establish a world class total car care shop, but what he gets from the neighborhood as a return on investment is not helping him achieve this goal. After much deliberation, he decided to relocate to a place that would appreciate his work and also pay for it, not continuing where even after many discounts some clients still end up owing and eventually not pay for services rendered. In his dream place he would be able to come up with his dream shop. How does he achieve this?

Chyke set up a two-year plan to raise money for a good shop and site in a middle-class neighborhood. He began to work and set aside a portion of his income to enable him make needed payments and purchase important tools and equipment the move would require. Sometimes strategy and realignment may require self denial of comforts or personal sacrifice and discipline for the individual to achieve his or her goal. Chyke understood this. He has cut down more than half of his personal spending except for things that are extremely important and absolutely necessary. He plans to continue this way until that goal is achieved.

It took Jesus thirty good years to prepare for a three year ministry. That was why He succeeded very well. He took time to know what His mission was and how to go about it. You discover that when He began the ministry nothing could stop Him; nothing was lacking. He was just living out the script. There were no issues like, "I did not know this will be like this... or ...that this thing or that will crop up." He was just on the go, and today He has been highly exalted by the father – The Almighty God. Anywhere Jesus is mentioned, victory becomes imminent. He is honored.

Taking time to think and plan concerning your endeavors and visions are very important if your goal is to succeed in those missions. Some see it as a waste of time and resources; however the reverse is the case. There is a saying that when we refuse to plan, we are already planning to fail. So planning helps you achieve your goals and dreams by reducing ambiguities and stress. Therefore, stop sitting there staring at the goals, arise, strategize and see yourself ahead in life.

For one longing for change in life, your life first needs to change to be able to attract those changes you crave. You cannot keep doing the same thing and expect to see something different. If you have not been strategizing before, perhaps that is why there have not been successes in the things you do. This happens when you act out of emotion and do not think things through before taking action. Try planning and strategizing today and see if it will not bring some changes in your endeavors.

Chapter III
You Must Be Strong

If you must succeed and win in whatever endeavor you choose to embark upon, you have to be strong and have great guts. Any football team or athlete that desires to win a prize in any competition or important event must train hard to develop enough muscle and stamina to succeed. He must also develop some skills as some sports require great techniques. In addition, the individual must be determined to perfect his skill set. This is very essential. These conditions are also what you desperately need in your pursuit of life's dreams and goals.

Strength is that hidden energy and character inside a person that keeps him working or going until he begins to see the result of his efforts. It does not matter the duration the result takes to show up, he remains on track – waiting. He does not quit.

Apostle Paul advised us (those that believe) not to throw away our confidence, which he said would pay off in the future if we persist and continue in whatever we do.

"Therefore, do not throw away your confidence, which has a great reward. For you have need of endurance, so that when you

have done the will of God, you may receive what was promised."
(Hebrews 10:35-36)

This advice is relevant to every sphere of our lives and in whatever vocation we find ourselves. You have to believe that you will succeed in your mission, difficulties notwithstanding. Your determination not to throw in the towel is a testament to your faith in the outcome of your efforts. You can apply this understanding to any field of life – business, politics, academics, ministry, marriage or discovery. Every successful individual is said to have a large reservoir of this force or energy within them, and that is one of the secrets of their success. They persevere! They do not chicken out or give in to opposition or hard conditions. They stand their ground and refuse to back down until they succeed and receive what they want. Sometimes you may need to go beyond patience to succeed. Some people endured many tests in order to achieve their goals.

The moment an individual allows this virtue (strength) to run out, the person crashes inside and runs into problems. After this, the next thing you hear will be, the individual is packing up and quitting his pursuit. What is this telling you? It shows that in addition to other important factors, strength is a virtue of great essence one definitely needs to succeed in anything he does.

Strength Can Be Obtained

In the book of Daniel 11:32, the Bible says that those who know their God shall be strong and do exploits. From this passage, you will discover that the knowledge of God is what strengthens the believer. When that knowledge strengthens him, he can then translate that knowledge into achieving great things. Also in Acts of the Apostles 20:32, the scripture says that the word of God is able to build you up and give you your rightful place among the sanctified. The strength you receive from this knowledge is what carries you along when difficulty and trials hit you as you pursue your goals. This energy keeps you going until you begin to see tangible results towards your expectations. In Psalm 23, David attested to this truth.

"The Lord is my shepherd; I shall not want. He maketh me to lie down in green pastures: He leadeth me beside the still waters. ...I shall fear no evil." (Psalm 23:1,2 & 4 [KJV])

The knowledge of God and His word boosted David's confidence to the extent that he believed that come what may, no matter the conditions he found himself, God was in charge. He was sure that God was able to work out every situation that came his way to his favor. David expressed that confidence with this declaration, *"...I shall not want."* (I have everything I need - NLT). This knowledge made him so sure of God that he kept pressing forward even when he had not seen the final results. His belief was that the end would be greater than his present situation. He knew the role of a shepherd to the flock and walked in that understanding. From his experience, every shepherd wanted good pastures for his sheep. He then compares that with the character of his own shepherd, God. God is a good shepherd and he trusted that God would do much more than any human shepherd.

This truth also applies to other areas of life. When you discover that God can be depended upon to supply your needs, then you need no longer fear, but place your confidence in Him. This found confidence is what gives you assurance in Him in your life's journey, and to say "bye-bye" to worry.

This strength can only be acquired by reading and studying the word of God, and living your life according to the word. The Apostle Peter in his epistle (2 Peter 1:2) prayed that grace and truth be multiplied to us through the true knowledge of God and of Jesus our Lord. It is through God's grace as we study and practice the word of God that we obtain this strength. Our daily dealing with God helps us understand Him more. When you wake up in the morning, you pray and ask for His guidance and direction. At the end of the day, you see you had a hassle-free day unlike if you had not committed the day unto His hands. You get sick and pray according to the word of God believing you will be healed; eventually you will be healed. You need something that looks naturally impossible, after fasting and praying with close communion with Him, you discover the problems solved. This is how to know God. It keeps going on and on, from one level to the other as you put His word into practice. There are times in which God may require you to do some things. Go ahead and follow His direction, this is obedience. As you keep training yourself like a sportsman, eventually you get to the point of great strength and stamina where you can now compete in the big leagues. This is how to acquire the strength that comes from God.

Another way to be strengthened is through hearing His word. The bible says that faith comes by hearing the word of God (Rom. 10:17). I think that is why Apostle Paul charged all believers that we should not neglect the fellowship of the brethren as is the manner of some (Heb. 10:25). When the people of God come together to worship, a lot of revelations, a lot of insights, and many ministrations take place that you may not ordinarily receive when you worship alone. At this place God uses others and the experience they had encountered with Him to open your eyes and also open you up to His truths. If we consider what Apostle John said in his epistle – 1 John 1:3 - 4, we will understand it better. He said,

"...what we have seen and heard we proclaim to you also, that you also may have fellowship with us; and indeed our fellowship is with the Father, and with His Son Jesus Christ. And these things we write, so that our joy may be made complete."

These truths are the things that strengthen you to keep forging ahead as you pursue life and your dreams.

Beloved, knowing God is very critical in one's path to success. Find out God's opinion about your dream, vision, pursuit or idea. The opinion you discovered is what will strengthen you as you pursue that vision. Hold on to those truths you discovered. He will surely bring them to reality. Whatever He has said concerning that goal, that expectation, that desire, He will make happen. What you are expected to do here is simply be steadfast and not faint. God promised never to leave nor forsake you. I tell you, He cannot lie (Hebrews 6:8).

A time came in the Bible, from Isaiah chapters 40 – 66, when God began to reveal His person to the people of Israel. They were losing faith in Him, seeking to get help from idols rather than the Almighty God. At that time God began to reassure them, strengthening their confidence in Him once again. It is a common saying that knowledge is power. Getting the knowledge of God today will get one empowered for great exploits.

How to Know God

Psalm 34:8 says, ***"O taste and see that the Lord is good: blessed is the man that trusts in Him."***

To determine how delicious a meal is one would have to take a bite out of it. This principle also applies to knowing the Almighty God. One knows and proves God when he spends quality time in His word daily and puts to practice the truths he discovers from His word. As one obeys and acts on the instructions, God responds. His response reveals more about Him. Oftentimes God's promises have conditions attached to them, and you discover that the moment you play your own part, God will not hesitate to respond. As one discovers this and other principles, he will begin to progress in the midst of difficult challenges along his way to success. When this is done, before he realizes it, he has reached his goal.

I thank God for the man God used to counsel me when I was newly born again. I call him my father in the Lord. During the days of my early development I would go to him for prayer and also listen to his wise counsel. Then one day, I think three days after I got born again, he refused to pray for me when I came to listen to him. He told me that I could pray for myself and God would hear me. Here are his words to me, "The love God has for Jesus is the same love He has for you. Whatever He can and will do for Jesus, that will He also do for you." I was surprised. I asked, "Are you sure?" He nodded his head and said yes in affirmation. He went on to say, "You need to bathe yourself in the word of God. Whatever He asks you to do, do it. Whatever He asks you not to do, abstain from it."I tell you the truth; that was the turning point in my life. God began to show me many things from His word as I devoured the scriptures. He equally gave me the grace to do them and have the real life experience of asking and receiving from God.

I shared this to let you know my initial encounter with God and how I came to know Him. You can know Him also and create a personal relationship with Him, and He will begin to deal with you in a more intimate way.

Source of Knowledge and Strength

Every person pursuing a career, a goal or dream should first conduct research with regards to it. The information gathered will help him know how to go about being successful in that field and industry. This also will help to identify possible problem areas and plan on how to tackle them as they show up along the way. However, it has been discovered that no matter how much effort you put into gathering your information, research may not uncover all of the details. Sometimes due to limitations in human knowledge and other factors, all variables may not be found.

However, it has been discovered that everything you need in life is in the word of God. The Bible is God's word. It has been found to be infallible in all areas of life. In many circumstances and situations people have tried to prove it a lie, but it has remained steadfast in being true; it has never failed. The Bible is filled with God's promises and other life principles. A careful study to discover the hidden gem and the strength deposited within is what reveals the power and wisdom of God hidden in it.

It was this strength that Abraham relied on that enabled him to wait till his promised son was delivered. He waited twenty-five solid years before this happened. It was his knowledge of God that helped him wait this long. I do not know any ordinary human who would have done that if the hand of God was not in it. The Bible also records that his wife, Sarah, had gone beyond childbearing age, but he was not deterred in his faith. Abraham's knowledge about God's faithfulness helped him stay strong during the trying period of waiting. He was not discouraged by the reproach and taunting from neighbors, friends, relatives and associates during this period.

From Abraham's experience, you will discover that a closer walk with God in humility, obedience, righteousness and truth will help you discover Him, and obtain the promise you seek after. Until one relates with another he cannot confidently and authoritatively say he knew the other person. However, a close look at Hebrews 11, which is known as the "Hall of Faith," will give you insight into those who knew God. They walked with Him. They knew the will of God and thus how to please him. They were at peace with Him despite what they saw on their way. They never wavered in their trust in Him.

These heavenly "Hall of Famers," unreservedly trusted God for all their expectations. They never doubted Him because they knew Him and what He could do. Eventually, they were not disappointed. Divine strength or supernatural strength is released to us when the Holy Spirit begins to reveal God to us. You discover that with this strength you can now do what ordinarily you could not have ventured into doing. However, without the true knowledge of God, you will run out of strength and quit.

Chapter IV
The need for Courage

nybody who must achieve set goals or dreams in life must, among other things, be courageous. He must have the heart and attitude for success. It takes a strong heart to succeed in life and in any chosen field. Without courage you will be intimidated or harassed out of the way by forces of this life. Courage means being fearless in the face of danger and never retreating in the face of daring oppositions. Some people do not realize that their dreams, decisions and steps may place them into dangerous situations. I want you to know this is possible, but you need a courageous heart to keep going when such circumstances arise.

When God called Joshua to lead the people of Israel to the Promised Land after the death of Moses His servant, He charged him to be strong and courageous. He knew that a series of challenges would come up along the way. Disheartening things could compel Joshua to quit or turn back. So, God charged him to be courageous, meaning that he should not entertain any fear even when it became difficult to move ahead.

God assured him of His continued presence and support at
every point of the way (Joshua 1:9). This assurance emboldened
Joshua and boosted his faith and confidence. If you remember,
Joshua served under Moses. He saw how God blessed Moses as he
carried out his divine assignment. Can you imagine what was going
through Joshua's mind when God transferred to him the same
assignment and assured him of His continued presence? Even though
he knew it would be tough and challenging, he was neither
intimidated nor overwhelmed by the enormity of the work. He
witnessed God's power and faithfulness towards Moses when he was
in command of the Israelites. He never saw God disappoint Moses at
any point he called on Him. As these experiences played through his
mind, as he ruminated over them, he became more confident and
bold and convinced he was equal to the task. Joshua knew that he got
the best backing any leader would need for that kind of assignment.
As a result he made up his mind to carry out the mission with
success. An Igbo adage (Igbo proverb) says, "A child whose father
sends on a mission is not afraid of obstacles to accomplishing the
mission."When the child knows he has his father's back, he throws
all his weight into whatever the mission is. He sees the father as a
defense and source of strength and inspiration. To him, the situation
must respect the authority and influence of the father. The child sees
the father as the ultimate guarantee of his success and having the
potential to deal with anything negative that may come up. So it was

with Joshua when God assured him of His presence and support. The Bible states that at last he succeeded in the mission.

For us today, God has given us the same assurance in all our endeavors. All we need do is arm ourselves with His promise and hit the gas; not looking back until the mission is accomplished. Do you know what will happen to you when you see God's promise fulfilled in your life? It will boost your morale. It will make you trust Him more and to take appropriate risk knowing that you will get the best of the situation. God is no respecter of persons. What He said to one, He says to all. What He says He will do, that He will do. He is not man that changes with time or people. He is just and full of integrity. All through the ages and times, He has backed His word with corresponding results. Psalms 89:34 and 12:6-7 attests to this:

"My covenant I will not violate, Nor will I alter the utterance of My lips." Psalm 89:34(NASB),
"The words of the LORD are pure words; As silver tried in a furnace on the earth, refined seven times. Thou O LORD, wilt keep them; Thou wilt preserve him from this generation forever." Psalm 12:6-7(NASB)

If you can trust Him like the people of old and begin to act on His words today as they did, you will begin to reenact those awesome miracles of old. You will begin to record extraordinary favors and breakthroughs in business, academics, politics, and more.

A friend of mine a couple of years ago went to China from the US on a business trip. In China he lost his travel documents including his cash. You can understand what that means. In fact he was stranded. He did not know what to do. At that time he had not become a US citizen to qualify for assistance from the US embassy at Beijing. However, he got a nudge to seek help there. There, he was asked to get an affidavit to show he lost his documents so as to be given a new travel document back to the US. He did not have any money left for that, nor did he know anyone that would be of help. The official he met said they could issue him one, but the fee was thirty dollars. This was equivalent to what the Chinese charge Americans to obtain one. Even that amount was too expensive for him but he had to do something. As he contemplated leaving the embassy in disappointment, he realized that the previous night his business representative there in China had given him a hundred dollar bill. He pushed through his pocket and found that the money was still there! A sense of relief came. He went back and handed over the money so he could get the paper processed and receive his change. Lo and behold, the money was counterfeit! This was like adding salt to an injury. At this time, the US was cracking down on counterfeits and people running the illegal transaction. Reports had it that North Korea prints US bills to enable them to do business outside their enclave.

To make matters worse, he is a Nigerian. Nigerians are not respected by many Western people. This disrespect and in some case dislike is perhaps due to the corrupt activities of a few, a very insignificant minority, who would sell their soul to make money. He was now fighting against government policy, negative attitudes, and a financial crisis all at the same time. There were alerts everywhere. He called his lawyer to inquire about the issue. The lawyer said it would take about a year to resolve. Another said six months. The embassy said they would need one month to thoroughly investigate the issue and get back to him. Meanwhile, he was in a country where he knew no one well enough to seek help. The thought of staying in China for a year without work or money was an impending nightmare. However, he had peace of mind. He knew he was innocent and did nothing wrong. He believed God for help. By this time he knew that the only help and savior he had was God. He began to engage in midnight prayers. According to him, he told God he was not afraid. If that was the way God wanted him to relocate to China, he was open to it; but if it was the devil or anyone else trying to manipulate or undermine him, it should not work. He said to God that He should intervene and glorify Himself through the incident. He prayed this for a couple of nights. One night, perhaps the third night, he dreamed that he received a phone call to come and pick up his travel documents. He awakened and began to praise God. That same day he received a call from the embassy to come and pick up his travel documents. It did not take one month, not six months or one year to resolve as he was told. It only took faith in God. Today this guy frequents China and his business is booming there.

Courage can take us to any length and height. It helps us to see success where people see failure. It helps us see a way where people see difficulties, see opportunities where people see only problems. It helps us to see obstacles as stepping stones to great things. Even when things are designed to damage and destroy us, the way we handle them will determine the outcome. That is why courage matters.

The problem is that we usually allow human logic to rob us of God's blessings. Some may ask, "How can I be successful when I don't have the right connections?" However when you have the Holy Spirit as your guide, there is no limit to what you can do. There is a wealth of potential lying idle in you that needs to be released, but its release depends on you. That is why you need a word like this to awaken you to step out, shake yourself, your faculty, and dare to make a mark and change your world.

You may ask yourself what Joseph read or studied after he was sold as a slave by his brothers. What connections did he have? However, look closely at his life story and you will discover that his dream of becoming the leader of his people was fulfilled despite all human efforts to undermine him. Conspiring to put him into the pit and selling him off into slavery could not stop Joseph's motivation. Even the long years of servant-hood and confinement in prison could not stop that ambition or dream. Courage kept Joseph's dream alive. Eventually, he became a prime minister in Egypt and when his people came over to join him during the famine in Canaan, he ruled over them, thus, fulfilling that dream. It was Joseph's courage and loyalty to God that brought his dream into fruition.

Unlike Joseph, a lot of people have disempowering core beliefs, and until they change them, they will continue in a vicious circle of self-depravation. They usually think that something must go in a particular way or it cannot work. You need to subdue your thought pattern to enable it to be aligned to what God is saying concerning you. The word of God is food to the soul. When you take in a lot of this word and saturate your mind with it, you begin to build some spiritual energy and confidence within. You will no longer be pushed here and there, from one corner to the other. You will know your rights and what belongs to you as a believer. With that, you begin to take some uncommon steps with uncommon results following. There is a great and wealthy place God has planned for you, but it takes heart to get there. Let us be like Caleb and take hold of our inheritance. Let us not be like other leaders of Israel who were pessimists and perished in the wilderness without seeing the land of promise. An Igbo adage says, "Onye kwe, chi ya ekwe." It means that God will never be an obstacle whenever you decide to do something good.

Believers should understand that the God who gave them their dream has placed within them what it takes to accomplish it. You do not need to look outside for it. All you need to do is to sit down and discover the power within yourself. Dwell in your dream (brood, incubate, visualize) until you are able to literally see it; develop your dreams and you will see yourself fulfill them. There is a brother I know. He is an automotive engineer. When he is working on a difficult task, he takes time to look at it. He begins to think about it and then to figure out what to do. He does not get panicky when an answer does not come immediately, neither does he solicit help from any. He analyzes the entire process in his head. He keeps at it until the idea strikes. At that time his face beams with a smile.

This has helped him do many car repairs. In fact some of his colleagues and dealers bring him their difficult jobs.

When the angel of the Lord identified Gideon as a mighty man of valor, he answered and said, "Who, me?"

"And he (Gideon) said unto him (Angel of God), Oh my Lord, wherewith shall I save Israel, behold, my family is poor in Manasseh, and I am the least in my father's house." Judges 6:15 (KJV)

A lot of us today are like Gideon and need to be told who we are in God. But the moment he took courage and obeyed God, he became what God purposed him to be. I do not know what your dreams are or what God is asking you to do, but I want to let you know that as God was with Joshua and Gideon during their own mission, so is He with you today. They had blood flowing in their veins like us today. Those guys were born of women and had one head like us today. They had their various weaknesses, but when they heard God, they believed and trusted Him. They took steps and therefore succeeded in their mission. You can too. It is the same God, the same Holy Spirit, the same Word and the same world. Those testimonies did not occur in heaven and were packaged for us to read here on earth. They were men and women too, like us. I encourage you to get the heart, begin to take some steps, and I bet you will see results. That thing they call "challenge" cannot kill you. Dare it by initiating and taking steps towards your idea and vision. Press on again and again. See, you are already there. I know you will make it; just get out of that cloak of fear. It does not help; it limits you.

There was a moment in history when the nation of Israel was heading towards a national humiliation from their enemy – the Philistines. No one had the courage to dare face the champion of the Philistines - Goliath. But when it came to the knowledge of the shepherd boy, David, he volunteered to challenge the Philistine.

I want you to learn some good lessons from David. When he went out to fight Goliath, David did not start considering his inabilities and his constraints. He did not consider Goliath's years of experience and his exploits as a soldier. He neither considered his small stature and youth a disadvantage nor his lack of military training. However, he concentrated on his credentials and his resume. He forgot about all he did not have and centered on the things he had. He remembered how God helped him kill a lion and a bear at different occasions, and rescued his sheep. He never took those for granted. He understood that it was God who gave him such victory. That made him count on God when a bigger challenge appeared in the form of Goliath and he won.

"Thus David prevailed over the Philistine with a sling and a stone, and he struck the Philistine and killed him; but there was no sword in David's hand. Then David ran and stood over the Philistine and took his sword and drew it out of its sheath and killed him, and cut off his head with it. When the Philistines saw that their champion was dead, they fled."1 Samuel 17:50-51 (NASB)

People do these exploits through the knowledge of God and the assurance of His ever abiding presence with them that motivated them into such daring acts. They were convinced that despite the situation they found themselves in they would surely overcome. These are the people we are considering here. You can be the next to be written about if you face your circumstances daringly.

There are other people in the Bible who also challenged and changed their world through courage. They stood for God and their belief even at the peril of their lives. They challenged the king to his face when he wanted them to offend their God, and he did his worst and threw them into fire. However, this act attracted the best of God for them. These people saw the King of Glory before He came to save mankind. That is the result of courage. I am talking about Shadrach, Meshach and Abed-nego. Their faith and courage shook the foundation of Babylon.

"Shadrach, Meshach and Abed-nego answered and said to the king, 'O Nebuchadnezzar, we do not need to give you an answer concerning this. If it be so, our God whom we serve is able to deliver us from the furnace of blazing fire, and He will deliver us out of your hand O king. But even if He does not, let it be known to you, O king, that we are not going to serve your gods or worship the golden image that you have set up.'"

The king became furious and ordered them to be thrown into the furnace of fire. However, after a time, the king had this observation.

"He (Nebuchadnezzar) answered and said, 'look! I see four men loose and walking about in the midst of the fire without harm, and the appearance of the fourth is like the son of the gods.'"
"Therefore, I (King Nebuchadnezzar) make a decree that any people, nation or tongue that speaks anything offensive against the God of Shadrach, Meshach and Abed-nego shall be torn limb to limb and their houses reduced to a rubbish heap, inasmuch as there is no other god who is able to deliver in this way. Then the

king caused Shadrach, Meshach and Abed-nego to prosper in the
province of Babylon."Daniel 3: 16-18, 25,29-30 (NASB)

Friend, He is still the same God as He was yesterday. He has not changed and will never change. He remains the same – complete and perfect. The Bible says He is from everlasting to everlasting. You can prove Him now. Taste Him and see that He is good. He can be depended upon.

What is that thing you want to do that you keep putting aside or shifting forward, or the one you are already doing that has kept you fearful? I charge you today to get up and begin to challenge that goal. Begin to dare it. The Bible testified in Mark 16:20 that when the disciples went out (began to take steps) the Lord was with them confirming their words (and actions) with signs following. A step of faith will make you see God surprise you.

The father of a young man, Alex, threatened to stop paying his tuition in 1988, during his second year in the university because the young man embraced Christ (was born again). The man demanded that his boy renounce his new found faith if he must continue to enjoy any benefit from him, or else, let God provide for him. Alex refused to renounce his faith and was not moved by the threat. He resolved rather to be sent packing from school than renounce the faith or deny Christ. As you well know a battle line has been drawn. Alex went back to school with the little supply his mom could provide without anything from his dad. Things began to change. Hardship set in with lack and deprivation, but Alex was firm in his faith. He refused to back down. After a year, his dad saw that he was not moved by his threat and that the young man was not feeling any pain or lack as he expected. So, during his third year in the university, his father threw him out of their home. Instead of that weakening Alex's love for God, it motivated him the more to get closer to God. According to him, it was an honor to suffer for Christ's sake. After his third year, God opened the favor gates of heaven and blessings began to rain. Alex concluded his studies and graduated from the university. It was while in the compulsory National Youths Service Corps program that his father got to know that his son made it and graduated from the university. He regretted the actions he took toward his son. Despite the lack of support from his father, Alex made a bold statement with his courage and defended his faith not minding if he lost his career.

During this trying period, former Nigeria's military leader, President Ibrahim Babangida introduced and approved bursary awards for all university students nationwide. Alex's department also got included to begin to receive I.T.F. or Industrial Training Fund money for its students that engage in industrial training. Through these opened doors and favor from brethren and friends, Alex was able to complete his university career. He accomplished this mission through sheer courage. At the end he not only gained a degree from the university, but he also kept his faith, and through him his entire household was introduced to Christ.

Like Alex, when you dare your circumstances, you overcome them. But if you allow them to intimidate you, they overshadow and keep you irrelevant. You are born to solve problems and change your world, so do not quit. God is counting on you to deliver that change. He has given you all you will ever need to accomplish your dreams. You have the word of God, you have the Holy Spirit, and also you have Jesus Christ backing you up every step of the way. You need to stir up the lion in you and hit the road. I tell you a good result is awaiting you. Stop idling the engine.

Chapter V
Determination

Determination can be described as a resolve from the inside to keep going until one achieves his or her desired goal. It is, not being discouraged by the numerous challenges and difficulties that usually come up along the way to accomplishing a dream. When you are feeling discouraged, your motivation is usually the result you hope to achieve at the end of the process. This expectation kind of numbs the effects and pains of the difficulties you encounter along the line. Determination is a deliberate choice to keep holding on until one begins to see light at the end of the tunnel.

A young man reportedly said, "Only death, and nothing else, can stop me from reaching my goal."According to him, as long as he was determined, obstacles and diverse challenges were not enough to stop him. All they can do he said is slow him down from his normal frequency and velocity.

When we consider people that have succeeded in their endeavors, their success stories have been traced back to their resolve and determination to succeed. If you examine the paths they went through, you will discover they were laden with thorns; but these people kept going. They preferred dying in the process rather than giving up in the process. But the truth is that they ended up not dying but being celebrated for great accomplishments. This has been their hallmark. You can put your name among these great people only if you can convince yourself you can. Another thing you need to do is close your eyes and senses to a deluge of obstacles that could come up and may want to sweep your feet out of the ground as you make a move. When you get to the second point you are ready go.

Take a look at Queen Esther. When she had not understood the purpose for which God sent her into the palace, she was content just being the queen. She was not willing to take any risks that might have jeopardized her position in the kingdom. I guess she just wanted to sit there and fill herself with the goodies of life. Maybe that might have given her relief and consolation for the death of her parents. But thank God for people like her uncle – Mordecai, who spoke to her strong words and made her realize her purpose for being in the palace. God sent her there to influence the deliverance of her people. When Esther realized this vision, she resolved to take action and accomplish the task even at the risk of her life. She sent her uncle to help her do this:

"Go assemble all the Jews who are found in Susa and fast for me; do not eat or drink three days, night or day. I and my maidens

also will fast in the same way. And thus I will go to the king, which is not according to the law; and if I perish, I perish." Esther 4:16 (NASB)

From this statement we see another Esther, a determined woman, who has set her eyes on a goal. Her determination made her commit her life to it – either I succeed in this mission or I die there trying. It is like a statement by the hungry four lepers in the book of 2 Kings 7:3-11. It is better to die trying than die doing nothing.

After fasting and praying, Esther went into the inner court of the king unannounced and uninvited, but God caused her to receive favor before the king. In that kingdom – Persia and Medes, nobody entered the king's court uninvited; and the judgment was usually death, unless the king held out his scepter to the individual – a symbol of favor. Esther challenged this law; she did not die but received favor instead. She accomplished her goal, which she set out to do – saving the Jews from annihilation, a plan hatched by Haman, one of King Ahasuerus' high-ranking officials. After this, Esther became more distinguished in the land before the king and her own people. The Lord Jesus said that those that want to save their lives will lose it, but those that are willing to lose it for His sake will gain it back. Whenever we get committed to fulfilling God's will, we are risking our lives for His sake, but He said we will gain it back.

Determination is what helped Esther to save her people from the evil plan of Haman.

Also, during the time Judah was in captivity in Babylon, some Jewish youths of royal and noble descent were selected for training so they could serve in the king's court. They were apportioned rations from the king's table. However, Daniel considered the king's table unholy and inadequate, so he decided against being a part of that table. His reason for making this decision was to avoid anything that might come between him and his relationship with God.

"But Daniel made up his mind he would not defile himself with the king's choice food, or with wine which he drank, so he sought permission from the commander of the officials that he might not defile himself." Daniel 1:8 (NASB)

As you decide and determine to pursue a course, begin to identify the right steps to accomplish that course. You need to take time to find out more about the course you are going into. It is very important. The Bible makes us understand that we should first and foremost get knowledge as we embark in any form of war. As long as Daniel was indecisive about the king's table, it never occurred to him to seek any permission to abstain from it; but when the right decision was made, the right actions followed.

This implies that determination helps produce ideas and actions to achieving your set goal. As long as you are indecisive you will keep seeing obstacles, but once you arrive at a decision, you will begin to see light at the end of the tunnel.

The scripture has it that at the end of the training, Daniel and his three friends excelled above others. Determination is what helps you excel where others fail. The storm that consumed others is the same storm that will push you to your wealthy place. Most stars became what they are today by not allowing obstacles and challenges to stop them; rather they overcame their obstacles by challenging them. Dare to be determined today concerning anything you want to achieve and see yourself achieving it. Do not just sit there looking at what you do not have; look at what you have and what you can do with what you have. Utilize what you have and take the proper steps. Before you know it, you will have a testimony and begin to tell your story. Break the dormancy over your life; it is a robber. Begin to move in line with your goal and forget about possible problems you may encounter. The truth is that every problem usually provides solutions to itself. Some people say, "Necessity is the mother of invention." If our inventors had waited to see a perfect condition before they started discovering things, we might have still been in the Stone Age today. But they dared to challenge their environment. They determined to make a change when they got tired of the norm. Today, almost everything has gone hi-tech. Can you imagine life without electricity, cars, aircrafts, schools, hospitals, telecommunications and computers? You cannot make a change without determination.

Today in Nigeria, you cannot say much about the country without mentioning the likes of Dr. Nnamdi Azikiwe, Obafemi Awolowo and Abubakar Tafawa Balewa to mention a few. It was sheer determination that made them get independence for Nigeria. If they had considered the sufferings, deprivations and other things that would be on their way to this great feat, they would have as well played the "good boys" to their colonial masters and continued serving them. But they knew the benefits of being independent, and so with their lives and strength they pressed for freedom.

In the Unites States of America, Dr. Martin Luther King, Jr. and other civil rights campaigners fought relentlessly against racism and inequality. Their determination and concerted efforts helped pave the way for equality among the races and end racial discrimination in government establishments. It has also led to an improved level of respect for human rights in the US. For anyone wanting to succeed in any endeavor, there is no option to determination.

Sometimes you hear people talk about "Plan B." They say if "Plan A" does not go well, they switch over to "Plan B." I think that when one is strongly determined to getting "Plan A" to work, there may not be a need for "Plan B."

It is the fear of obstacles that usually gives birth to "Plan B." However, with strong determination I do not think it would be necessary.

I remember the story of a young boy from my town in those days when education was not so popular. His name was Chris. He grew up among seven boys of the same parents. He happened to be the last child of his parents. He wanted to attend school and gain some education, but Chris did not have the means; his father was dead. According to the custom, he began to serve his eldest brother whose name was Jerry, who in turn began to support him. At the time, Jerry was a palm produce merchant. He took Chris along to make the purchases. Sometimes the job was assigned to him alone as his elder brother found him diligent and faithful. Chris continued with his brother in the trade, but his interest for school refused to die. He kept combining trading and schooling. On market days – which was usually on special days he would go and make the purchases. Whenever he returned from the market, he would leave for school. The report had it that the boy was brilliant. At the end of his primary school career, the young man passed the then standard six certificate exam with distinction. He also passed the admission exam to attend high school at the then Merchant of Lights Grammar School, Oba in the former Eastern Nigeria.

Meanwhile, Chris had another elder brother – Silva, who was already in college at Dennis Memorial Grammar School, Onitsha in the same former Eastern region. However, Silva's high life style in school made it impossible for their eldest brother to consider adding Chris to his training plans.

Chris felt so bad and disappointed but determined to pursue his studies left the trade. His determination was tested when the eldest brother approached him and appealed to him to give up his dream and continue with him in the trade. Promises of things that mattered then were made to him, like getting him a bicycle, a wife, and a gun among other things. But these things did not appeal to Chris who was sold-out to going to school. Later, when he left Jerry another of his brothers – Steve, a transporter, began to support him, and Chris enrolled to do a correspondence course. The story had it that the little boy was so determined that he stayed at home, read, studied and passed the then prestigious London GCE Ordinary Level and Advanced Level examinations. He later joined the Nigerian Police Force in 1952. He received many awards of excellence from the force and rose to the rank of Superintendent before he retired.

Also before his retirement, Chris was accepted to study Law at Oxford University, London. It was his passion for education and determination that propelled him to pursue this feat. However, due to a lack of funds and the outbreak of the Biafra – Nigeria Civil War, he could not make it. The essence of this story is to help you see how far determination can take you in life. It does not matter how you began or started, as long as you are determined your end will be great.

After the war Chris concentrated on his career and raising his family. After meritorious long years of service in the force, he retired and became the Administrative Manager of an International Construction firm in Nigeria in 1989. He passed on in 1992.

Friends, you can achieve anything you want when you set your mind to it. Nobody can defeat you when you have not defeated yourself. There is a saying that goes, "Where there is a will, there is a way." It takes your willingness to hold on for you to see the results you want. Do not allow situations to cower you into humiliation.

That is not your lot. You are meant to be great and stay at the top. Stop crying for the devil; you are a child of God. Jesus said that ye are gods. See how Moses tormented Pharaoh and the Egyptians when they would not let the people of God go and serve Him (Exodus 7-11). Take your position and begin to torment the devil and his agents. The Bible says you should resist him and he will flee from you. Tell him no, enough!

Sometimes I see some sisters crying because they have not married, nor birthed children. I tell you wipe those tears away. Put your energy into serving God; begin to express your love to Him. He knows how to make those things available. When you commit yourself to His service, He will honor you. Jesus said the father will honor whoever serves Him (John 12:26). The Bible enjoins us to seek the kingdom of God first and all other things will be added to us, even those things unbelievers are dying to get (Matthew 6:33).

Chapter VI
Good Association

For you to successfully achieve your desired goals in life you need to be careful of the company you keep. One needs to be extra careful here because the company you keep determines among other things how far you can get in life. You need people of like minds, that think the way you think, feel the way you do, to really achieve your desired goals. You need people that will complement you and provide you with the things you do not have; people who will encourage, support and respect your views. You need those that will add to you those tonics that will spur you up; those that will motivate you positively when you get tired on the way. The Bible says that two are better than one. If one falls, the other lifts him up, and iron sharpens iron. It is also a common saying that two good heads are better than one.

There are dream killers, people who when you relate your dreams to them will kill them in a second. They only see obstacles and problems on the way. They will never encourage you to look beyond that obstacle. Such people will make you see a thousand and one reasons why you should be "wise" in your decisions.

I say it again; the people you associate with determine how far you can get in life (Proverbs 13:20). They also determine how fast or quickly you get things done.

When Moses was about to begin his military campaign against the inhabitants of Canaan to dispossess them of the land God promised the children of Israel, he first began by sending out twelve spies to search out the land. Although they set out on their mission, they returned with a negative report that killed the morale of the people. It affected the mission and the entire journey.

"So they gave out to the sons of Israel a bad report of the land which they have spied out saying, 'The land through which we have gone, in spying it out, is a land that devours its inhabitants; and all the people whom we saw in it are men of great size. There also we saw the Nephilim (the sons of Anak are part of the Nephilim); and we became like grasshoppers in our own sight, and so we were in their sight.'" Numbers 13:32-33 (NASB)

Some people are like the spies Moses sent out. They make a mountain out of a molehill. Any association with this set of individuals will see your dreams dead. That report was part of the problem the people of Israel had on the way to their dreamland. They became afraid as a result of the report and decided against going to war to take the land. This provoked and angered God because it was a vote of no confidence in Him.

This set of people sometimes are in the majority as we saw in the passage of the Bible we examined. The same thing is applicable to the church and society today.

However, there are still people who believe that God remains able, and will give them their expectations no matter the circumstance. Although they are in the minority, locate them and associate with them. In verse 30 of Numbers 13, Caleb, one of the spies rose up, and addressed the people. He said they were able to go up and take the country. However, because the believers were in the minority, they lost at the opinion poll.

This passage helps us understand the need to be informed and patient as we make choices of associates or even workers we want to work for us. During this process and time of making this choice for any purpose, one need to be able to discover good and true companions they can associate with in their pursuits. I want you to know that associates have a lot to do in your life; sometimes they determine your rising and your falling.

You need people who will complement your efforts and help your weaknesses, people who can give you sincere and quality counsel during your time of need and people who love your advancement. Take heed to avoid lazy and jealous people who drain you of your energy.

Jethro, Moses' father in-law, drew him close and counseled him when he noticed the young man was heading for leadership problems. Jethro's principles helped Moses fulfill his mission (Exodus 18:17-18). You need men and elders like that on your journey toward your dream. They will tell you the truth – they are not hypocrites. They are not just about what they can grab from you. These are pillars that you can lean on, not caterpillars that eat up resources. Find people who can help you nurture and build your dreams.

Also, you need friends or associates that are loyal, people that will like to share in your burden and your joy. You need people in the same fate as you. They understand the urgency and need attached to your pursuit and dream.

Let us take Daniel and his friends as a case study. King Nebuchadnezzar dreamt and forgot his dream. He threatened to kill all the wise men in Babylon, including Daniel and his friends, if no one was able to tell him the dream and its interpretation (Daniel 2). When Daniel got the information, he ran to meet his friends; they discussed the situation and immediately began to seek the face of God concerning the dream and its interpretation. It created an accord because they were in the same predicament and in need of God's help. They prayed and God heard. He revealed the dream and the interpretation to Daniel.

Locate people that are in the same fate with you, who are earnestly seeking a miracle from God, not people who are comfortable and cannot pray; who are not willing to deny themselves of little comforts. You need those who are determined to see results.

Sometimes, unfaithful brethren will tell you, "O brother, it is well with you. We are praying for you." Really…?! They are not praying for you. Those that may try will only make prayers that cannot pass the ceiling. If I may ask, how many times have they refused food and cried to God for your sake, asking God to help their friend or brother out of his problem and change his situation? Rather, they spend their time praying for their own needs. Some do not even remember you asked them to help you pray about a need.

Beloved, you need men and women who are hungry for results and change like you. Join with them; fervently pray together and encourage one another like the disciples of old. I tell you the truth, before you realize it, you will be face to face with your results.

Some people want to succeed in business, some in academics, others in ministry, while some in politics. But a lot do not know how to go about it. Others are still praying about it. You have to understand that you need to begin to associate with people you desire to be like if you will reach your goal. In Proverbs 13:20, the Bible says that if you walk with the wise you become wise, but if you are a companion of fools you suffer harm. If you want to become a business man begin to associate with business people and not just any business people. Look for those that have succeeded and associate with them. Before you realize it you will already have started thinking like them. It is important that believers look to business people who are of the same faith as they are and have become successful.

If your interest or calling is politics, the same thing is applicable there. You do not associate with classroom teachers or traders when your interest is to become a politician. It is necessary to associate with people of your chosen career or interests because iron sharpens iron. If you have the potential to become a politician then you should associate with others who have the instinct and skill of a politician. When you follow this advice you will easily find your footing. But if you go to an environment that is hostile to your dream, that dream will die. On the other hand, when you get to the ground where it is accepted, it will not only germinate, it will grow and flourish there. There is a saying that birds of the same feather flock together. You know what, when they flock together they warm each other up and generate some powerful energy.

Look for those who have succeeded in the field you are about to venture into. Associate with them and mine their wealth of experience; you will not be disappointed. It works in any area of life. If you want to be a great pastor associate with great pastors; if you want to be a successful wife, associate with successful wives, the same is true with husbands who want to have a successful marriage, associate with those that have successful marriages. If you want to be righteous, associate with righteous people. As students if you want to succeed academically associate with those who do well in academics; that is just how it works. This means you have to dump some and take up other relationships and associations if you want to achieve certain things. Your destiny and reach are in part tied to the kind of association you are involved in. Today is still early; you can make up for any lost time.

Chapter VII
God's Presence

"Thou will make known to me the path of life; In Thy presence is fullness of joy; In Thy right hand there are pleasures forever." Psalm 16:11 (NASB)

Whenever you decide to pursue a goal or get involved in one project or another, you discover that what helps us navigate the intricate paths is usually God Himself who through His presence provides us with the steps to follow to get the job done without much tears. You may well know that at times when you begin some projects, it is like troubles are let loose. They begin to manifest in one form or the other.

The peace, the joy, the ability and creativity you need during troubling times come when God's presence is available to you. God's presence brings an unexplainable assurance and peace to the believer inspiring him to keep going and remain hopeful. What may lead others to commit suicide or quit will just look like a piece of cake to him or her. If we remain faithful to Him, God has assured us of His ever abiding presence and grace as we navigate life.

"When you pass through the waters, I will be with you; and through the rivers, they will not overflow you. When you walk through the fire, you will not be scorched, nor will the flame burn you." Isaiah 43:2 (NASB)

Life happens. There are also so many things that accompany life. There are lots of uncertainties and disappointments. Challenges do occur in diverse ways as people pursue their dreams, but God enables us to defeat them as they come, through the things He teaches us as we navigate the rough paths. That is why His presence has been of immense importance in every life's journey.

Sometimes God Himself bears our burden. I am always fascinated by the "Footprints in the Sand" story by Carolyn Joyce Carty. In that story she portrayed how God comes into our situation to carry our burden. The story is about a man who dreamed he was on the beach taking a walk with the Lord. Across the sky flashed scenes from his life. For each picture he noticed two sets of footprints in the sand; one belonged to him while the other, the Lord. As the last scene appeared, he noticed that many times along the path of his life there was only one set of footprints. This, he observed, happened during the hardest and saddest moments of his life. The discovery bothered him a lot and he questioned the Lord. "Lord, you said that once I decided to follow you, you'd walk with me all the way. But I have noticed that during the most troublesome times in my life, there is only one set of footprints. I don't understand why when I needed you most you would leave me."

Then the Lord replied, "My son, my precious child, I love you and I would never leave you. During your times of trial and suffering, when you see only one set of footprints, it was then that I carried you. "

This story is a clear example of how the Lord deals with us as we pursue life and its goals. He has not changed except that we have usually sidelined Him when wanting to solve life our way. Numerous sad stories have resulted due to this. Many people who tried some of the same difficulties that you went through and succeeded, never survived it; others committed suicide along the way. The difference here is the presence of God. You definitely need His presence every step of the way in all your pursuits. Moses knew the risk of going without God in an adventure and so he refused to continue the journey to the Promised Land if God's presence would not go with them.

"Then he (Moses) said to Him (God), "If Thy presence does not go with us, do not lead us up here. For how can it be known that I have found favor in thy sight, I and Thy people? Is it not by Thy

going with us, so that we, I and Thy people, may be distinguished from all the other people who are upon the face of the earth?""
Exodus 33:15-16 (NASB)

This episode occurred after the people of God committed idolatry; God became unhappy with them and opted out from accompanying them in the journey. However, Moses understood the implication of God not going with them on that torturous journey. God's presence provides them security; He provides the direction. He knows when to change course. Moses was not comfortable gambling without God so he interceded on behalf of His people and waited on God to change His mind and continue with them.

Eventually He did and the journey continued. Do not try to do anything without God accompanying you. It will be too heavy and risky for you, and you will end up paying a great price for it. The advantage of God's presence while traversing life's journey cannot be overemphasized. The sad experiences of others as they go through challenging situations will not be the same for you because God will be with you to knock off every obstacle and bogeyman along the way. The Bible says in Psalm 91: 7-8, that *"A thousand may fall at your side, and ten thousand at your right hand; but it shall not approach you. You will only look on with your eyes, and see the recompense of the wicked."*

What they mean in essence is that those evils that usually destroy men and women along the way cannot reach you. Your protection is guaranteed by His presence. Verse four of the same chapter says, ***"He will cover you with His pinions (feathers), and under His wings you may seek refuge; His faithfulness is a shield and bulwark" (NASB)***

I encourage you, beloved, to take out time and study Psalm 91 in your closet. It will help you understand and discover more about the power of His presence. You definitely need God's presence to overcome life struggles.

Contacting God's Presence:

The Bible says that without faith it is impossible to please God. And he that comes to Him must believe that He is, and that He is a rewarder of those that diligently seek Him (Hebrews 11:6). It also says if a man purges himself of all these (sin and all unrighteousness), he becomes a vessel of honor prepared for the Master's use unto every good work (2 Timothy 2:21).

When one takes steps and time to consecrate himself or herself to God, that individual begins to attract the presence of God.

In the book of James 4:8, the Bible says when you draw near to God, He will draw near to you. He requires you to cleanse your hands and purify your minds by His word. After that He wants you to remove unbelief and double mindedness, then the rest is done by Him.

In Genesis 35:1-6, when Jacob consecrated his entire family as he was relocating from Shechem to Bethel, the presence of God descended mightily upon his entourage, and they made it safe. The Bible has it that the presence of God prevented the surrounding cites from attacking him and his family as they moved. Before his camp received this awesome company see what Jacob did:

"So Jacob said to his household and to all who were with him, "Put away the foreign gods which are among you, and purify yourselves, and change your garments,"; …So they gave to Jacob all the foreign gods which they had, and the rings which were in their ears; and Jacob hid them under the oak, which was near Shechem"(NASB)

What I discovered here is that the moment the people obeyed, the presence of God descended among them, and they walked in safety to their destination.

A close look at the issues dealt with by this company will show you how they made it. They dealt with issues that took their minds away from God *(...foreign gods...),* and purged their hearts *(...from unforgiveness and other issues that pollute their minds...).* They also put away all unrighteous deeds and forms *(...change your garments...).*

Joshua did the same thing when he was about to cross the people over to the Promised Land. They needed God and His supernatural power to cross over the River Jordan.

"Then Joshua said to the people, "Consecrate yourselves, for tomorrow the Lord will do wonders among you.""Joshua 3:5 (NASB)

Consecration is a mark of brokenness. If one goes further to walk in line with God's instructions and tremble at His word, he will begin to command more of His attention and presence. God loves humble and devoted people. (Isaiah 66:2)

Chapter VIII

Focus

Someone said you cannot be looking up and down at the same time. You cannot be going northward and southward at the same time. Either you are going north or you are going south. If not, you are going nowhere. You are just making a movement, lots of noise without impact. If you try you may end up stumbling assuming you are walking or someone may think you are crazy. Jesus said, "You cannot serve two masters at the same time." Either you favor one and defraud the other, so is the issue of focus. In fact, without focus you do not make a meaningful impact in life. You become a rolling stone that gathers no moss. I remember one of those days when planting a church in the city of Warri – Nigeria. There was this gigantic warehouse we rented. It was well constructed with concrete blocks and cement. However, there was a leak at one of the ends – a small leak. I observed that whenever it rained, there would be drops of water that usually take a second or so to hit the floor. Drops continued to land on that same spot of the concrete floor. I suppose it lasted as long as the building existed. What fascinated me was that as small as the force of these drops were, they created a hole in that concrete floor. This is a floor that you may need a dynamite to blow up because it will take you donkey hours if not days to use hand tools to break it up. That is the power of focus. I remember reading a magazine article in 1998, or so by my beloved bishop, David Oyedepo. In that he said, "Anything that stops you from daily taking steps to your desired goal has stopped you from reaching it forever." Since then this statement has remained in my consciousness because he was talking about how paramount the force of focus is in the success of any endeavor. I have seen a lot of people after starting a venture, they hear another story, and they quit to begin something new while not finishing the one already started. Some have opened many businesses or started schools but with nothing to show for them after many years. Sometimes they think it is the devil attacking them; no it is not. It is your lack of focus in what you are doing. The Bible says that my people are destroyed for lack of knowledge. Begin to give attention and focus to all you do and see a good difference. Make it a rule if not a law for yourself to always finish whatever you start no matter how foolish that may sound in another's ears.

This is the problem a lot of people have in relationships too. Instead of giving attention and focus to their relationship, they think quitting the current person and escaping the situation is easier and will save them a headache. Then they rush into a new relationship. This is no solution. That is why you see them running from Peter to Paul, from Agnes to Naomi without having a settled and successful life.

Know what you want, give it all you got, your energy, passion and time. I bet you will see a big change; something you will be happy and proud of. I know a lot of people want ready-made everything, but there is nothing already made anywhere. You are to make or create what you want and deck it the way that appeals to you.

Many people who are accomplished in life are people with a single vision. They are not people who try this today and tomorrow they are over there. They are people who have tenacity and consistency. They have a vision of where they are going and what they intend to accomplish. Look at some of these names in the scripture – Jesus Christ, Apostle Paul, Abraham, Moses, Elijah and others. They were successful and accomplished their missions. They never allowed distractions to lure them away from their vision.

In our contemporary society today, we have people who through the singleness of vision or focus, conquer the world in their own areas. In information technology we have people like Steve Jobs, Bill Gates and Mark Zuckerberg. It is not their wealth that made them outstanding but the power of their focus to change the world and how it works. It is the product of this focus that gave them the wealth and all the recognition they enjoy today.

In US politics, you have the Kennedys. They are good in public service. They have produced generations of public servants in this great country.

In sports, we know about Jackie Robinson, an American baseball player who became the first African-American to play and succeed in Major League Baseball. We also have the likes of Tiger Woods, Serena Williams and Tim Tebow among others. All these people, if you look at their success stories, they centered mostly on the discipline of focus.

Focus also helps you discover some vital points and links to what you are looking for. Those in sciences will bear witness here. If you want to discover what is causing someone fever, the lab technologist usually gets samples of the patient's specimen. Sometimes they collect the urine, feces and blood. Some drops of these samples are viewed under the microscope to determine the parasite. However, the technologist has to focus the lens on the prepared slides to enable him or her to identify the causative agent.

Focused people are not easily discouraged or intimidated in their pursuits. Rather, they will always see a way to get around the obstacle to obtain what they want. Their eyes are always trained to be on what they want – the spoil. A good place where you can see the force of focus at play is among successful farmers. Sometimes after an unsuccessful season where the harvest is poor, instead of giving up they are not at all deterred. Their focus is usually on the next planting season on how to make it work, and on how to get a great harvest at the end of the day. That is what matters to a farmer. Their mind-set is success; they only see success and not the obstacles. They find a way to deal with things that want to contradict their view – success. If you are close to them you will discover their diligence when the planting season is fast approaching. They engage massively in clearing the farmland even before the coming of the first rain. Some will go further to till the ground to make sure the land is good enough to allow rain water or irrigation to sip into the soil to soften it for planting seeds. After planting, they check the young plants for pests, and they kill any found feeding on them. After a time, they weed the farm to take away unwanted plants to ensure the plants were not choked competing with weeds. Too much competition could result in reduced crop yield. After the weeding time there is also a session of mild tilling to allow more water access to the root of the plants to enhance growth and crop yield. The farmer also uses the same diligence during harvest. There is also the waiting period and the growing stage of the crops. The farmer waits patiently expecting.

If you look at the entire process, it is full of work, but the farmer only sees the large harvest awaiting him. At the end you discover his dream coming true; joy that knows no bounds filling him due to the bounty. This is usually the experience of every focused individual embarking on any meaningful venture in life. As long as the person is focused and not derailed by distractions he or she will make it to the end.

There are times after working so hard to succeed you find yourself at a crossroad; not of your own making but things beyond your control. It is at this point also that one needs the force of focus to maintain and achieve balance and set goals. Take for instance you got laid off from a job, not because of your incompetence, but rather you were terminated wrongly in a job unceremoniously due to envy that led to a setup and eventually resulted to dismissal. It could be so devastating, especially when you still have so many things waiting for you to do; or it may not be job related, but an issue of life very important to you that could be humiliating and discouraging. At this point you definitely need focus to get ahead and not put down your head in shame or regrets.

With focus you see yourself bounce back. Your detractors would be wondering how you were able to beat them. But once you descend to self pity, you lose the ground and the vision, even the energy to pursue would be drained. I would like us to look at a few examples of people who beat all odds to achieve greatness. They employed the force of focus and determination to achieve their dream.

If you read Genesis 26:14-22, the story was about Isaac. In the preceding verses God blessed him greatly in the land where he sojourned after he obeyed Him by sowing in that land. However, that was the beginning of his troubles. Out of envy and fear the people he domiciled with ejected him from the land and closed the wells the father Abraham built in the time past. In modern times it could mean destroying his father's assets – estates or businesses. I am not going fully into the story, but his attitude when this incident occurred. When he received the quit notice from the king of the land, he left the place to another location. In the new place he began to reopen his inherited closed wells. As he tried, the Philistines quarreled and claimed the wells; but he did not let go. He dug another; the same thing happened. At this time he went away from the Philistines and dug another well, but they did not quarrel over that any more. Can you see that? Isaac wanted to succeed; he was not deterred by their opposition. He only chose to change location so as to achieve what he wanted.

A lot of people are like Isaac who out of envy and jealousy or fear and abuse of power were sacked from where they abode and made a living. Others are in the same predicament today due to business failures owing to wrong investments or other crisis. But a look at Isaac will help us handle such conditions very well. Isaac did not begin to pity himself or start accusing his enemies. Rather he kept his eyes on the mark. All the tricks, all the provocations, all the assaults and distractions did not deter him from being who he was. He continued pursuing his course. He was able to achieve this because he was determined and focused. Perhaps you are down somewhere. Get up! Remember where you planned to go before you fell. Dust up and continue the journey. Stop crying. It does not help you; you only beat yourself up emotionally. You may need to change a trade if what you currently have is not helping you fulfill your dream. Or you may have to change locations as Isaac did, or change friends or partners to reach your goal. As long as you have the drive and focus, you will get to your destination.

Former American president, Abraham Lincoln, who so many refer to as the sixteenth was a man who wanted to succeed in life, and he did despite numerous challenges he passed through in life. Today he is celebrated as a great leader. If you look at his life and career, they were filled with lots of pot holes, but he gave it his best and the rest has been history. He had many setbacks and obstacles in life; in romance, career, health, politics, but he was not deterred. He kept pursuing life and success.

In politics he failed several times. His fiancée died and he got depressed. For about six months he was hospitalized. During his presidency he encountered many more challenges – led the nation to war. There were many other things that did not go well in the life and career of this great man. But his driving force was success and he was focused on achieving that in whatever he did. Even though he failed to win some elective post at some point, he did not give up on himself or that vision. Eventually, he became a US president of great repute. Most of us when things do not go the way we expected once or twice, we quit. For more than twelve times he had serious setbacks in things that mattered to him in life, but he did not quit. At a time, although he had to remove himself from contest after seeing the writing against him on the wall because of his position on an issue, he bounced back later. His eyes were on the spoil and eventually he got there. These are mortal men who have flesh and blood running in their veins. If they could so focus, determine, and succeed in their endeavors, what stops us from replicating the same thing or even doing more and better things in our own time? Let us take a cue from them. They were bold, determined and focused. Eventually they achieved their dreams.

Also, today a lot of us are enjoying different types of amenities, things that are making life easy. These are products of relentless efforts of our inventors, people who do not like the status quo. They love change, good things and life not filled with hardship and sufferings. That is why this set of people took it upon themselves to keep discovering things that would ease life. They have kept at it with many results to show. They are doing this because they are focused on bringing good to humanity. Some of the challenges and oppositions they meet along the journey did not discourage them in any way. They always found a way to overcome the obstacles and achieve what they wanted. You can imagine what an airplane looked like when the Wright brothers first invented it. But today they have become a classic. You have got different categories that move everywhere – transatlantic and local. They help ease travel in comfort and time. Focus is what got us to this level when you compare it to how it was at its inception. The inventors and those that followed after them kept working at it to bring out its beauty and value. They never allowed the obstacles they encountered along the way to discourage their advancement. Eventually we are where we are today because of that. The same thing will happen when we refuse to quit on our pursuits. Despite the obstacles, the beauty will eventually show up if we are focused and if we persist.

CONCLUSION

Reading this book is evidence to you that God loves you. This book is another testament of God's acts among men. He has not ceased attending to issues of concern to humanity. Also He has not ceased to be interested in you and all that concern you. So, as you read this book, take a moment and ask yourself in sincerity, "Have I really made peace with this good God?"

If you are not born again and reading this book, perhaps you are having a series of challenges in life but will like to have a permanent freedom and succeed in life. First you need the Lord Jesus Christ in your life today. Stop running your life yourself before you wreck it. Jesus can take you through life in victory. The Bible says that those that are born of God overcome the world.

"For whatsoever is born of God overcometh the world: and this is the victory that overcometh the world, even our faith." 1 John 5:4 (KJV)

We are born again when we realize we are helpless sinners bound for hell without Christ, and when we voluntarily receive Christ into our lives as Lord and Savior by confessing and renouncing our sins and inviting Him into our lives.

"But as many as receive Him, to them gave He the power to become sons of God, even to them that believe on His name." John 1:12 (KJV)

If this is your choice, take this prayer with me after confessing your sins before God.

"Lord Jesus, come into my life, be the Lord of my life. I accept you today as my Lord and Savior. Thank you because I am born again. Amen."

Congratulations my friend! God bless you. You are welcomed into the kingdom of God today. You need to begin a walk and relationship with God. First you should locate a Bible believing and Holy Ghost filled church and fellowship group in your locality. Once you have done these things, join in with your new found Christian brothers and sisters and begin to worship with them. You should also make sure to attend the mid-week and weekly programs of your new Church family.

For inquiries please email: don't_quit2000@yahoo.com

Again, God bless you. Know this; life is not complete without Christ – Shalom!

DON'T QUIT!

The Bible says that those that press enter the kingdom. Jesus, underscores this in the book of Matthew 11:12, charged the church not to be complacent. ***"And from the day of John the Baptist until now the kingdom of heaven suffereth violence, and the violent take it by force."*** Therefore brethren, let us not allow things that are meant to be under our control stop us from achieving our goals in life.

www.ingramcontent.com/pod-product-compliance
Lightning Source LLC
Chambersburg PA
CBHW071904020426
42331CB00010B/2669